You Are Not Crazy

How To Heal From Your Couch

THERAPY WORKBOOK

Laurie Ford

COUNSELING AND CONSULTING

You Are Enough! How to Heal from Your Couch Therapy Workbook

Copyright © 2019 Laurie Ford, LPCA

Independently Published
ISBN: 978-1798299067

All rights reserved. This book contains material protected under international and federal copyright laws and treaties. Any unauthorized reprint or use of this material is prohibited. No part of this book may be reproduced or transmitted in any form or by any means, electronic or mechanical, including photocopying, recording, or by any information storage and retrieval system without express written permission from the publisher except in the case of brief quotations embodied in critical articles and reviews. This book is for information and educational purposes only. Please consult with your therapist for official therapeutic advice.

ACKNOWLEDGEMENTS

Thank you to my Lord and Savior, Jesus Christ, for speaking the vision of this workbook into my life. Thank you Lord, for giving me the courage to complete this assignment. Thank you to my wonderful husband, Eddie, for his love, support, and encouragement. Thank you to my sister, Zakkia, and friend, Sharhonda, for your love, empowerment, and suggestions on this project. Thank you to my two amazing aunts, Sharon and Janet, for your continuous love and support throughout my lifelong journey. Thank you for being mother figures in my life. Thank you to my lifelong mentor Judith for always being there and allowing God to use you as a mother figure in my life.

INTRODUCTION

Healing Starts With You

Taking time out of our schedules to see a Mental Health therapist isn't the most popular approach in today's society. However, seeing a therapist is one of the best investments you can make in yourself. Nurturing your mental health is just as important as your physical and spiritual health. When you invest in your healing, your legacy will reap the benefit of no longer being affected by cycles of trauma.

Being one of seven children born to a drug addicted mother, and not knowing my father, life wasn't exactly easy. Experiencing anxiety and depression as a teenager, and later, as a college student, was challenging to say the least. One of the ways I survived was through reading self-help books. Self-help books gave me the motivation and courage I needed to move forward with my purpose. The books enhanced my self-esteem during the years I didn't hear encouraging words from others. Throughout my journey I realized I didn't choose the life I was born in, but this was the life that was given to me. I figured I could either complain about it or make a difference. I chose to be bold and make a difference.

This workbook was a vision from God. I was asked to create this workbook to break the barriers between effort and excuses. I am very aware that there are people dealing with internal pain but lack the confidence to seek help. Don't worry. I wrote this book for you. Today is your day. You can heal from home as you work through this workbook. Invest in your mental health by taking the time to work through these exercises. You won't regret it. This therapy workbook will allow you to begin the healing process from your very own couch, reversing any preconceived notions you may have had about seeing a therapist. The actual work starts with you, so why not start today? Congratulations! You're one step closer to internal freedom.

TABLE OF CONTENTS

Let's Began With You 1
Mindset Shift: Your Actions Start With Your Thoughts 3
Self-Confidence Toolkit 4
Mirror, Mirror: What Do You See? 7
Acknowledging The Truth About Me 9
Getting Outside of Your Comfort Zone 13
What Are You Carrying In Your Suitcase? 14
Social Media Prison 16
Choosing Popularity Over Purpose 17
Removing The Social Media Mask: Identity Theft 18
What Can I Control? 20
You Were Made To Be Unique 21
Owning My Life 22
I Am Enough: Positive Affirmation 24
Self-Care Tips 25
My Personal Permission Slip 26
To The Little Girl/Boy Inside of Me: Part 1 and 2 27
Create Your Own Story 29
Healing Is In The Letters 30
Forgiveness 32
Reflection 33
Living My Best Life With Goals 34
Moving Forward With The Three C's 36
Who Am I? 37
Congratulations! You Made it! 38
Bonus Reflection Questions 39
Finding A Therapist 40
Bonus Page 41
Meet The Author 42
Encouraging Words 43

Let's Begin With You

It takes courage to ask for help and support. The value of your health goes beyond just your physical body. Your psychological, emotional, and social health are equally as important. We all face obstacles that may result in challenges related to one's mental and emotional health. Allow yourself to be open and honest during each section of this workbook. You deserve your best self and it all begins with YOU.

In this section write down everything that has hindered you from working towards the life you want to live.

What current emotions are you experiencing in your life?

_____
_____
_____
_____
_____
_____
_____
_____
_____
_____
_____
_____
_____
_____
_____
_____
_____
_____

Who or what is in the way of achieving your goals?

_____
_____
_____
_____
_____
_____
_____
_____
_____
_____

What are your distractions?

_____
_____
_____
_____
_____
_____
_____
_____
_____
_____

Mindset Shift:
Your actions start with your thoughts

Change starts in the mind. In order to change your behavior, a shift in mindset must take place. Your mind can't become comfortable with negative thoughts. Complacency should have no place in your mind. Healing can only take place once you acknowledge what it is that you need to heal. Stand in your truth concerning your feelings and actions. Below are questions that will help you begin changing the way you think. The questions will help challenge your mind to look at obstacles differently. Remember, you have everything you need already in you to move towards the best version of yourself. You've got this! No more procrastinating. Change your thoughts and your actions will follow.

CHANGE YOUR SELF-TALK

How can you look at things differently? **Change your perspective**!

Looking at life from the lens of a positive mind state can add more value to your purpose! When you are faced with the day to day obstacles of life, reframe the questions you are asking yourself and watch the results change.

Below are new ways to ask questions and communicate positive internal thoughts during emotional hardships.

- What do I want my future to consist of?
- What am I responsible for?
- What are the facts?
- What am I assuming?
- How can I help?
- What could we lose?
- What steps can we take to improve the situation?
- What's possible?
- What do I want?
- What am I missing or avoiding?
- What's there to accept and forgive in myself and others?
- What can I learn from this person or situation? From this mistake or failure? From this success?
- How can I make this a win-win situation?
- What action steps are the most logical?

Self-Confidence Toolkit

Everything you need is already in you. You are equipped to build your self-confidence by using the qualities in YOU.

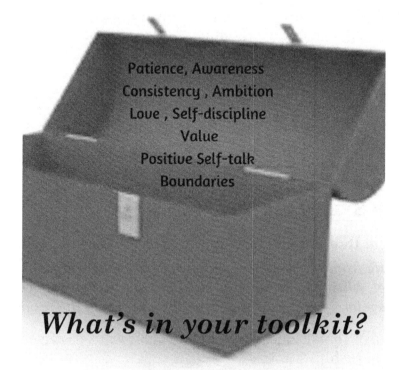

What are the things I value most?

_____
_____
_____
_____
_____
_____
_____
_____

What are my top strengths?

_____
_____
_____
_____
_____
_____
_____
_____
_____
_____
_____
_____

Make a list of things you are grateful for.

_____
_____
_____
_____
_____
_____
_____
_____
_____
_____
_____
_____

During what part of my life have I had the most success?
Note: Success isn't limited to your career or income, it could be anything you've achieved such as knowledge or happiness.

_____
_____
_____
_____
_____
_____
_____
_____
_____
_____
_____
_____
_____

What motivates me? What are my hobbies?

_____
_____
_____
_____
_____
_____
_____
_____
_____
_____
_____
_____

Mirror, Mirror: What do you see?

How do I see myself?

_____
_____
_____
_____
_____
_____
_____
_____
_____
_____
_____
_____
_____
_____
_____
_____

How does the world view me?

_____
_____
_____
_____
_____
_____
_____
_____
_____
_____

Acknowledging The Truth About Me

In order to start the healing process, acknowledging your truth must come first. Ignoring your feelings will hinder the healing process and make it impossible for your mindset to change. In the section below, write down what has contributed to any current unhealthy feelings and actions. Use these questions to begin to acknowledge your inner feelings.

Write about your insecurities. What are they and where did they come from?

_____
_____
_____
_____
_____
_____
_____
_____
_____

Who or what contributed to your pain?

_____
_____
_____
_____
_____
_____
_____
_____

How did your childhood contribute to any mistakes or regrets you've experienced?

_____
_____
_____
_____
_____

Who did you depend on for guidance and financial support in your life?

_____
_____
_____
_____
_____

How do you feel about yourself? What does loving yourself consist of? What do you do to show yourself love? What actions show a lack of love?

_____
_____
_____
_____
_____

In this section, you will complete the sentences below with your thoughts and feelings.

If you really knew me, you would know _____

_____

I've overcome obstacles such as _____

_____

As a child I dreamed of _____

_____

My life today is _____

_____

My support system consists of _____

_____

I believe in _____

_____

In the workplace I value _____

_____

Family is _____

_____

Self-care to me consists of _____

_____

The person I value the most is _____

_____

When I feel overwhelmed I _____

_____

I wish _____

_____

During the day I spend most of my time _____

_____

It's hard for me to _____

_____

My religious beliefs contributed to _____

_____

Getting Outside of Your Comfort Zone

Your comfort zone is actually the product of being uncomfortable. The only reason you feel comfortable in this place is because it brings a sense of familiarity. Your greatest moments take place when you are uncomfortable and outside of your comfort zone. The emotion of fear shows up and pushes you to reach your goals. Staying stuck in comfort can delay your goals. One of the biggest mistakes that we make is making our comfort zones bigger than our desired goals.

Today, I want to challenge you to get uncomfortable.

In the smaller square, I want you to write down what's in your comfort zone and in the big square I want you to write down things that are out of your comfort zone. Use this time to dig deep.

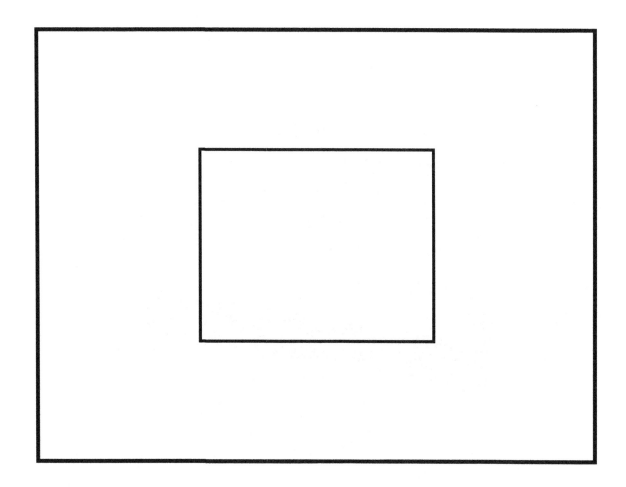

What are you carrying in your suitcase?

Oftentimes, when we don't want to face the truth about our pain, fears, and guilt. We pack our proverbial suitcases and "keep it moving." We go through life faking our identity just so we can function in society as what is deemed a normal person. Sometimes, keeping it moving is something that we've inherited through generations. Other times, we are running away from ourselves, not realizing this is impossible. You can never run away from your pain. Instead, we tend to carry the pain like a heavy suitcase. You carry this suitcase not realizing that as life goes on, you add more to the suitcase by not dealing and healing. After years of carrying around unhealed emotions, the suitcase is now weighed down with bricks and layers of hurt, shame, guilt, fear, abandonment, rape, abuse, low-self-esteem, etc. In this section write down everything you've carried in your suitcase and why.

Write about the dead weight you would like to take out of your suitcase.

_____
_____
_____
_____
_____
_____
_____

In the suitcase pictured below, write down the positive emotions you want to add to your suitcase. (Example: joy, peace, etc.)

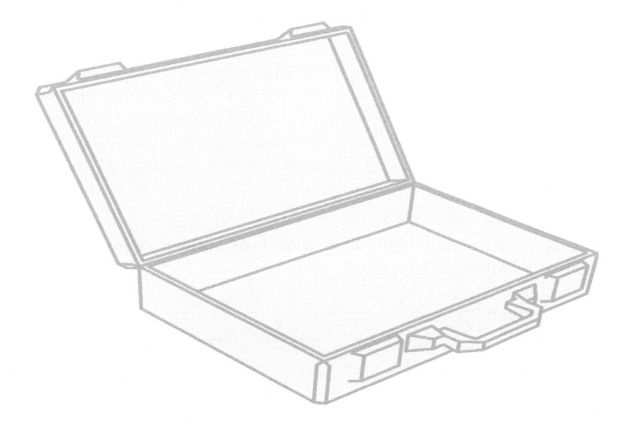

Social Media Prison

Social media today has influenced our thoughts, behaviors, and self image. Social media plays a vital role in the increase of anxiety and depression symptoms. Seeking validation from strangers has become the new norm in our society. What happened to finding your purpose and confiding in friends, family, and mentors? If you aren't careful, spending too much time on social media will rob you of taking steps towards who you were called to be

In this next section, write about how social media influences your life in both a negative and positive way.

_____
_____
_____
_____
_____

Choosing Popularity Over Purpose

The choices you make play a vital role in what you become. You have a right to choose the path that will lead you in the right direction. Choosing to be popular is a decision we've all made at a point in our lives. However, reflecting on that choice usually delays making it to your purposed destination. Conforming to what's popular is easy, but it's not worth losing out on who you really are.

In this section I want you to complete the sentence with what you will choose over popularity.

I will choose _____ over popularity.

I will choose _____ over popularity.

I will choose _____ over popularity.

I will choose _____ over popularity.

I will choose _____ over popularity.

I will choose _____ over popularity.

I will choose _____ over popularity.

Remove The Social Media Mask: Identity Theft

Until you stand in your truth, your voice will remain silenced. The words you speak won't be heard because you are speaking from the place of a broken identity. Sometimes we portray an image of who we would like to be or who we admire on social media. We cover our true personality with a mask.

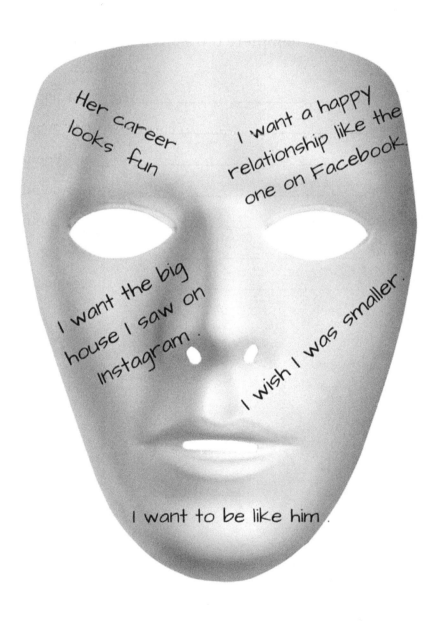

In this section, I want you to take the mask off and write a letter to the person who's been hidden for months, years, or weeks. Be honest and speak to the reason you've been hiding behind an image that wasn't created for you.

Dear (Insert Name)_____:

I am not being true to myself on social media because,

_____
_____
_____
_____

Sometimes I wish _____

_____
_____
_____

As I began to heal and start this new journey, I will no longer hide who I am called to be. Hidden my true identity is no longer an options for me. I will begin to love who I am and be grateful for my journey.

Love Always,

_____

What can I control?

Anxiety symptoms happen when we feel we have no control over our lives. There are things in life that are in our control and things out of our control. Fix your focus, in this section, to zone in on what you can control. Below is an example of what you can control. After reviewing the example write four more things that are in your control.

I can control _____.
I can control _____.
I can control _____.
I can control _____.

I Cannot Control

I can't control others opinions.

I can't control my past.

I can't control the family I was born into.

I can't control _____.
I can't control _____.
I can't control _____.
I can't control _____.

You Were Made To Be Unique

You are unique. The way you were born is exactly who you are supposed to be. Conforming to the way other people think and act can be damaging to your life's purpose. Do you ever wonder why you think differently from your friends? Do you ever wonder why you don't have a huge group of friends? I have the answer: You were made to " FIT OUT." You have a mind of your own and you must use it. Sometimes the people around you may show characteristics of jealousy regarding your accomplishments, attire, and appearance. When this happens, we began to dim the light in our lives. We stop working towards the person we were created to be in order to please other people. I encourage you today to let your light shine. You are exactly where you should be in this season. Your life matters! Think about the things that make you happy. Think about what brings you the most joy. Let your light shine while doing these activities. Be comfortable with who you are. Be bold and be ready to "FIT OUT."

Take a moment and reflect on the times you followed the crowd, although your mind was telling you not to follow anyone. Write about your experience.

_____
_____
_____
_____
_____

In this section write about what makes you different from others.

_____
_____
_____
_____
_____
_____

Owning My Life

Throughout this new journey in life, you must take the necessary steps to own who you are. Taking complete ownership of who you are and where you want to go helps you to focus on your journey. This section will bring you one step closer to owning who you are.

> *Owning your difference may feel lonely, scary, and hard at times. We were all created for a different purpose and owning the uniqueness of our image gives us "POWER."*

What does it look like to you to own your difference? Explain in detail.

_____
_____
_____
_____
_____
_____
_____

What should I nurture about my outer appearance that I've neglected? Why?

_____
_____
_____
_____
_____
_____
_____

What dreams do I have that I'm afraid to start working towards?

Am I trying to fit into the vision of others?

"I Am Enough" Positive Affirmation

Daily affirmation can have a positive impact on your self-esteem. Positive affirmations are used to boost self-confidence. Sometimes the best encouragement comes from within. In this section fill in the blanks with uplifting positive words.

I am enough, and I have enough

I was created with a purpose.

I am unique.

I am _____.
I am _____.
I am _____.
I am _____.
I will _____.

I am in control of my happiness.

I am not my mistakes.

I deserve love.

I _____.
I _____.

I will inhale positive energy and exhale fear.

I am proud of _____.

I am allowed to say, "NO."

I will move in the direction of my goals.

All I need is within me.

I am Enough!

Self-Care Tips

My Personal Permission Slip

Giving yourself permission to let go of your current and past pain can be hard. Unhealthy emotions can be strongholds that hold you back from living a life of peace. Today, give yourself permission to let the past go.

I, _____, give myself permission to let go of resentment, anger, and pain. I give myself permission to forgive myself for:

_____
_____
_____

I give myself permission to forgive everyone who has hurt me in the past. I give myself permission to take ownership of my life. I give myself permission to take the proper steps to heal my broken heart and open wounds. I give myself permission to:

_____
_____
_____

Today, (Date)_____, I will began working towards the life I deserve to have.

Sincerely,

Name _____

Date _____

Signature _____

To The Little Girl/Boy Inside of Me

When you reflect on the little person inside of you, sometimes you realize you were missing things that weren't shown to you during your childhood. In this section, write to the little girl or little boy inside of you. Tell him/her what you wish you received as a child that you didn't receive. Be honest with yourself.

_____
_____
_____
_____
_____
_____
_____
_____
_____
_____
_____
_____
_____
_____
_____
_____
_____
_____
_____
_____
_____
_____
_____

To The Little Girl/Boy Inside of Me: Part 2

In this section, write to the person you are now, explaining how you will give yourself what you needed as a child.

Create Your Own Story

Your life may not be the life you dreamed of. You are responsible for your own happiness, accomplishments, joy, and peace. Maybe you thought you would have a new house, career, or car. Maybe you thought you would be married with children. Use this section to create your own life story. What would you change about your life? If failure couldn't happen, what would life look like for you? What would you do if you were able to start over? Use the space below to create your life story.

_____
_____
_____
_____
_____
_____
_____
_____
_____
_____
_____
_____
_____
_____
_____
_____
_____
_____
_____
_____
_____

Healing Is In The Letters

Write a letter to the person or people who contributed to your negative emotions. Tell them how the pain affected you. Remember, you don't have to write letters to everyone in one day. Take your time and start with one person at a time.

Letter # 1

Dear _____:

Letter #2

Dear _____:

Forgiveness

When we hear the word forgiveness, we tend to turn the other way. We avoid this word because we can no longer play the victim once we forgive. Forgiveness is healing for you, not the other person. Holding grudges and holding on to emotions dictates how we live our lives. Forgiving ourselves and others will help us grow. Before we can forgive others, we must begin to forgive ourselves. Forgiving yourself takes time. We must begin to reflect on past actions that have affected us in a negative way emotionally. Most of us have done things we weren't proud of. Sometimes we feel that if we had a better childhood, some of the mistakes would've never happened. The mistakes happened, but they are now in the past. The letter below will help guide you to forgiving yourself. Fill in the blanks where the letter allows.

Dear _____ *(Insert your name)*

I am proud of you for taking steps to heal. I know this process is hard, but you are getting through this. I am proud of you for taking the chance to no longer let the pain of your past affect your future growth. I know you've made several mistakes in the past including: _____
_____

I am not proud of them at all. At that point in my life I felt: _____
_____

If I could do it all over again I would, but I can't. I want you to know (Insert your name) _____ *that's it's ok to let the past go. Forgive yourself for past mistakes. You can't change them. You can only learn from them. You are smart, strong, and loved. You have the strength within to forgive everything you've done to contribute to your own unhappiness. From this day forward, promise to love yourself, treat yourself with respect, ask for help or guidance when needed, and learn to cope with your emotions in a healthy way. Thank you (Insert name)* _____ *for being brave and beginning to choose you first. Again* **"I FORGIVE YOU"**

Reflection

How did you feel when writing this letter of forgiveness?

Living My Best Life With Goals

CURRENT SHORT-TERM GOALS:

_____
_____
_____
_____

DEADLINE FOR GOALS:

_____
_____
_____
_____

GOAL MOTIVATION:

_____
_____
_____
_____

HOW WILL I ACHIEVE THESE GOALS?

_____
_____
_____
_____

Living My Best Life With Goals

LONG TERM GOALS:

_____
_____
_____
_____

DEADLINE FOR GOALS:

_____
_____
_____
_____

GOAL MOTIVATION

_____
_____
_____
_____

HOW WILL I ACHIEVE THESE GOALS?

_____
_____
_____
_____

Moving Forward With The Three C's

Consistency: Consistency is the landmark for the things you consider impossible. What you do on a daily basis will contribute to the success you desire. Consistency is the motivation that helps you continue to go after your goals. As you continue your journey of happiness, stay consistent.

Commitment: Make a commitment to put yourself first. Stay committed to living a life full of peace and joy. Set boundaries for yourself and others. Stay committed to working towards the life you want to have.

Courage: Life takes courage. It takes courage to become the greatest asset in your life.

In the box below write about how you will incorporate the three C's in your life.

Who Am I?

In this section write about who you are. If you were given the opportunity to talk to an audience about who you are, what would you say?

Congratulations! You Made It!

In this section write a letter to yourself celebrating your progress

Congratulations!

Dear (Name) _____

_____
_____
_____
_____
_____
_____
_____
_____
_____
_____
_____
_____
_____
_____
_____
_____
_____

You made it through the healing workbook. Taking the steps to heal can be uncomfortable, but your hard work will pay off in the long run.

Bonus Reflection Questions

How did you feel when first starting this workbook?

_____
_____
_____
_____

How did you feel after completing this workbook?

_____
_____
_____
_____

What was the best section for you in the book?

_____
_____
_____
_____

What was the hardest section of the book?

_____
_____
_____
_____

Finding a Therapist

- If you work for a company, ask the Human Resources department if they offer mental health services through your employer.
- Call your insurance company and ask about local therapists in your area.
- Ask your insurance company about your mental health benefits?
- What is your deductible and has it been met?
- How many sessions per calendar year does your plan cover?
- Does your plan require a referral from a primary care physician?
- Ask your insurance company about your copay.
- Remember the copay for mental health services are different from regular doctor visits.

ADDITIONAL WAYS TO FIND A THERAPIST

- www.psychologytoday.com
- Social Media (Instagram/Facebook/LinkedIn)
- Mental health events in your local area
- Ask your local doctors office and hospitals for a referral to a therapist

CRISIS HOTLINES:

- National Suicide Prevention 1-800-273-8255
- Free Mental Health Helpline 1-877-665-3492
- The National Domestic Violence Hotline 1-800-799-7233
- National Association of Addiction Treatment Providers: www.naatp.org

Bonus Page

DEPRESSION

Depression Symptoms	Coping Skills
Loss of interest in hobbies	Talk to a Therapist
Consistent sadness	Express yourself through writing, coloring, or painting
Continuous negative thoughts	Practice positive self-talk
Loss of appetite or overeating	Stay involved
Suicidal thoughts	Ask for help from others
Self-harm	Get 7 to 8 hours of sleep per night
Feeling hopeless, worthless, or helpless	Exercise or participate in any physical activity
Lack of concentration	Eat healthy

ANXIETY

Anxiety Symptoms	Coping Skills
Feeling agitated or angry	Journal
Racing thoughts	Listen to soothing music
Difficulty falling asleep	Deep breathing
Excessive worry	Find a positive distraction
Panic attacks	Create something new
Uncertainty	Participate in an activity you enjoy
The desire to control people and events	Meditating

Meet the Author

Meet Laurie Ford, founder and CEO of Laurie Ford Counseling and Consulting, LLC. As a Licensed Professional Counselor Associate, Laurie is dedicated to helping individuals discover the person they were purposed to be. Laurie holds a vested interest in finding healing through self-love, positive affirmation, and removing emotional barriers impeding one's willingness to move forward. She believes that you can design a life of healing, true joy, and freedom through obtaining both mental and spiritual balance. Born in Charles City Virginia, Laurie is no stranger to struggle and disappointment. She is confident that the many obstacles she's encountered throughout her life have qualified and fueled her desire to help others take the necessary steps to put themselves first, seeking optimal physical and mental health. Allow her to partner with you on your journey to mental health and wellness.

Author's Contact Information

Facebook page: *Laurie Ford Counseling and Consulting*

Mailing address: *125 Remount Rd. Suite C-1 #391; Charlotte, NC 28203*

Instagram: *_mrs.ford*

Psychology today: *https://www.psychologytoday.com (Laurie Ford)*

Encouraging Words

You are NOT a mistake. Obstacles will show up, but how you react to them speaks volumes. Remember, you are enough! Freedom comes through mental healing. Healing takes effort and hard work, you were built for this. From this day forward, I challenge you to continue the positive journey to invest in yourself.

Made in the USA
Columbia, SC
28 October 2024

44716946R00030